Sabbath Solutions

MORE THAN 350 WAYS
YOU CAN WORSHIP
ON THE LORD'S DAY

Sabbath Solutions

MORE THAN 350 WAYS
YOU CAN WORSHIP
ON THE LORD'S DAY

BY
TRINA BOICE

spring creek
BOOK COMPANY

PROVO, UTAH

ISBN: 1-932898-15-8
e. 1

Published by:
Spring Creek Book Company
P.O. Box 50355
Provo, Utah 84605-0355

www.springcreekbooks.com

Cover design © Spring Creek Book Company
Cover design by Nicole Cunningham

Printed in the United States of America
10 9 8 7 6 5 4 3 2 1
Printed on acid-free paper

Library of Congress Cataloging-in-Publication Data

Boice, Trina, 1963-
   Sabbath solutions : more than 350 ways you can worship on the Lord's Day /
by Trina Boice.
      p. cm.
   ISBN 1-932898-15-8 (pbk. : alk. paper)
   1. Sabbath. 2. Sunday. 3. Church of Jesus Christ of Latter-day Saints--
Doctrines. I. Title.
BX8643.S2B65 2004
263'.3--dc22
                              2004010549

TABLE OF CONTENTS

Most of us are familiar with one of the Lord's "Top Ten" Commandments: to keep the Sabbath Day holy. What does "holy" mean and exactly how do we spend 24 hours worth of "holy" day? The title *Sabbath Solutions* implies that there is a problem. The Sabbath Day isn't the problem but our ability to treat it as a holy day often is, especially if you're like me and have active children who simply can't be expected to sit still and read the scriptures all day or quietly reflect on the Savior for hours on end! Adults often think that such quiet activity is how to keep the Lord's Day holy, but there is so much more to this commandment than just that!

The Commandment

The commandment to keep the Sabbath day holy is found in the Bible, the Book of Mormon, and the Doctrine and Covenants, and has always been part of the gospel. Sabbath observance is an element of our faith and obedience to eternal principles. It is a sign, a test, and a blessing to the Lord's people. The Lord said, "It is a sign between me and the children of Israel for ever." (Exodus 20:17) Your spiritual lineage includes you in the group of the Lord's covenant people who are expected to observe this divine command.

The Sabbath was referred to in the Old Testament days as a blessed and hallowed day (Exodus 20:11), as a holy convocation (Leviticus 23:3), and as a day of spiritual celebration (Leviticus 23:32). If those words don't describe your typical Sunday then you need to keep reading this book! The Sabbath day is a gift to mankind from the Lord; a day to rest from the concerns of the work day and a day to bask in the spirit. Sunday is a day to nourish our spirits. I love the following expression: "We are not humans having a spiritual experience, but we are spiritual beings having a human experience." Sunday is a weekly opportunity to remember why we are here and to reflect on how we are doing.

The Lord consecrated the Sabbath as a day for remembering the great work of the creation. "And on the seventh day God ended his work which he had made; and he rested on the seventh day from all his work which he had made. And God blessed the seventh day, and sanctified it: because that in it he had rested from all his work which God created and made." (Genesis 2:1–3)

From the very beginning, God has instructed His prophets to teach the covenant people to honor the Sabbath day. Some people mistakenly think the commandment originated with Moses on Mount Sinai. Like the Lord's mouthpieces before him, Moses was presented with the commandment to give to the people, as recorded in Exodus 20:8–11:

"Remember the Sabbath day, to keep it holy. Six days shalt thou labour, and do all thy work. But the seventh day is the Sabbath of the Lord thy God. In it thou shalt not do any work, thou, nor thy son, nor thy daughter, thy manservant, nor thy maidservant, nor thy cattle, nor thy stranger that is within thy gates. For in six days the Lord made heaven and earth, the sea, and all that in them is, and rested the seventh day: wherefore the Lord blessed the Sabbath day, and hallowed it."

Jarom was the first to mention the Sabbath in the Book of Mormon. He explained that his people "observed to keep the law of Moses and the Sabbath day holy unto the Lord." (Jarom 1:5) When the people kept the commandments they prospered in the land. Sabbath observance is a divine law given to man to help him in his earthly walk. It is a part of the complete gospel.

Even the earth was given a Sabbath rest: "But in the seventh year shall be a Sabbath of rest unto the land, a Sabbath for the Lord: thou shalt neither sow thy field, nor prune thy vineyard." (Leviticus 25:4) The Lord wisely counseled that we are to bless and hallow the Sabbath day. He made it clear that not only are we not to work on this day, but we are not to expect even the stranger to work. Clearly, when we patronize any business on the Sabbath, we are part of the cause for a person having to work. In biblical times the commandment to rest and worship was so strict that violation of it called for the death penalty! (Exodus 31:15) Of course, physical death is no longer the penalty for desecrating the Sabbath; however, we can cut ourselves off from the Lord and bring a type of spiritual death upon us when we choose to disobey.

Later, when Moses was leading the exodus in the wilderness, the Lord miraculously fed the children of Israel by sending manna from heaven. He instructed the Israelites how to preserve the heaven-sent manna over the Sabbath day. The manna had to be gathered and used the day it fell, or it became wormy and would stink. (Exodus 16:20,30.) On the sixth day, prior to the Sabbath, twice as much manna fell as on the other days. (Exodus 16:5.) The children of Israel were instructed by the Lord to gather twice as much so that it would last for two days because the manna did not fall on the Sabbath day. When they did this, a third miracle happened. On the Sabbath day the manna gathered the day before did not stink, and there were no worms in it, for it was preserved for Sabbath day use. (Exodus 16:24) The children of Israel were physically taught how to observe the Sabbath, however they didn't understand the spiritual lesson of the manna. Let's not focus on what we can and can't do so much that we forget to center our Sundays on the true "bread of life" — Jesus Christ!

An Eternal Principle

Elder Bruce R. McConkie confirmed that Sabbath observance is an eternal principle, and he found five occurrences in the scriptures when it was required of the Lord:

- "From the day of Adam to the Exodus from Egypt, the Sabbath commemorated the fact that Jehovah rested from his creative labors on the 7th day." (Exodus 20:8-11)

- "From the Exodus to the day of (Christ's) resurrection, the Sabbath commemorated the deliverance of Israel from Egyptian bondage." (Deuteronomy 15:12-15)

- "From the days of the early apostles to the present, the Sabbath has been the first day of the week, the Lord's Day, in commemoration of the fact that Christ came forth from the grave on Sunday." (Acts 20:7)

- "The Latter-day Saints keep the first day of the week as their Sabbath...because the Lord so commanded them by direct revelation (D&C 59)."

- "Sabbath observance was a sign between ancient Israel and their God whereby the chosen people might be known. (Nehemiah 13:15-22, Isaiah 56:1-8, Jeremiah 17:19-27, Ezekiel 46:1-7)." (*Mormon Doctrine*, p. 658)

Both the Sabbath and families were instituted in the Garden of Eden, and in God's purpose they are perpetually linked together. Through the Sabbath, He preserves for the family an opportunity for communion with Him and with one another. By keeping the Sabbath day holy, as He commanded us, we show our love for Him and give recognition of His authority in our life. It is a weekly opportunity for us to show whose side we're on! It is a special time when we can stop the world, in a way, and focus on things eternal. The solemn command brought down from the thundering Mount Sinai has never been rescinded, but rather, reinforced in modern times.

A Holy Day

So how exactly should a "holy" day be different from one of our regular days? The American Heritage Dictionary offers six definitions for the word "holy":

1. **Belonging to, derived from, or associated with a divine power; sacred.**

   Not only does the Sabbath Day belong to someone divine, but so do you! Not only do you associate with a divine power when you spend the day in true worship and devotion, but you will receive divine power by doing so. Not only is His day sacred, but so are you. The Lord consecrated the Sabbath as a day for remembering the great work of the creation. Mankind was His finest creation. In a way, the Lord has set apart the Sabbath Day to also help us remember the wonder that we are and to revere this gift of life. It is a weekly reminder that our very lives are sacred.

2. **Regarded with or worthy of worship or veneration; revered.**

   Don't you think the Lord is worthy of more than the three hours of Church worship we often routinely offer Him? Are you spending that time in Church visiting with your friends in the hall or are you actually engaged in true worship? Does your Sunday behavior show the Lord that you revere Him? Would others also be able to see that by how you spend your day?

3. Living according to a strict or highly moral religious or spiritual system; saintly.

When we are baptized we make a covenant with Father to keep His commandments. When we go to the temple to receive our endowment we make even more covenants that show the Lord how willing we are to commit to Him and His kingdom. Shouldn't Latter-day Saints live according to a spiritual system that would, indeed, be described as "saintly"? The Prophet Joseph Smith said "Let us here observe, that a religion that does not require the sacrifice of all things never has power sufficient to produce the faith necessary unto life and salvation" (Lectures on Faith, 6:7). Our observance of the Sabbath is an indication of the depth of our conversion and our willingness to keep those sacred covenants.

4. Specified or set apart for a religious purpose.

Both you and the Sabbath Day have been set apart for a

religious purpose! "Pure religion" was defined by James "to visit the fatherless and widows in their affliction, and to keep himself unspotted from the world." (James 1:27)

5. Solemnly undertaken; sacrosanct.

These words could describe how the Lord created the world and all of His creations upon it. Would it describe your attitude and the way you spend the Sabbath Day?

6. Regarded as deserving special respect or reverence.

From the time we are young children in Primary we are taught to show respect and reverence towards such things as the temple, the Prophet, or even the chapel in our Church building. Once we get home from Church on Sundays it is often difficult to maintain that reverent feeling at home. The Sabbath doesn't end when you walk out of the Church building; it lasts all day!

A Blessing and a Promise

We can and should receive spiritual strength when we keep the Sabbath day holy. It's like one of those things in life where you get out of it what you put into it. Our families will also be blessed by Sabbath observance. So, what blessings are we promised with this commandment? Doctrine and Covenants 59 offers written promises that are similar to those found in Leviticus:

"Verily I say, that inasmuch as ye do this, the fullness of the earth is yours, the beasts of the field and the fowls of the air, and that which climbeth upon the trees and walketh upon the earth;

"Yea, and the herb, and the good things which come of the earth, whether for food or for raiment, or for houses, or for barns, or for orchards, or for gardens, or for vineyards;

"Yea, all things which come of the earth, in the season thereof, are made for the benefit and the use of man, both to please the eye and to gladden the heart;

"Yea, for food and for raiment, for taste and for smell, to strengthen the body and to enliven the soul."

Another promise is found in Isaiah 58:13-14, which reads, "If thou turn away…from doing thy pleasure on my holy day; and call the Sabbath a delight, the holy of the Lord, honourable; and shalt honour him, not doing thine own ways, nor finding thine own pleasure, nor speaking thine own words: Then shalt thou delight thyself in the Lord; ...for the mouth of the Lord hath spoken it."

Another purpose, as well as blessing, for Sabbath observance is to keep ourselves "unspotted from the world." Without the Sabbath, we could become so immersed in the world and its temporal concerns that we would fail to see the eternal nature of life's blessings around us. Keeping the Sabbath Day holy reminds us to keep an eternal perspective and allows us to reflect on how it is we're spending the other six days of the week. We are promised both temporal and spiritual blessings by simply keeping the command to keep the Sabbath Day holy.

President Ezra Taft Benson shared, "The purpose of the Sabbath is for spiritual uplift, for a renewal of our covenants, for worship, for rest, for prayer. It is for the purpose of feeding the spirit, that we may keep ourselves unspotted from the world by obeying God's command." (*Ensign*, May 1971, p. 4)

In the November 1986 *Ensign,* Elder James E. Faust offers three reasons why he thinks the Lord would ask us to honor the

Sabbath: "The first has to do with the physical need for rest and renewing. Obviously God, who created us, would know more than we do of the limits of our physical and nervous energy and strength.

"The second reason is, in my opinion, of far greater significance. It has to do with the need for regeneration and the strengthening of our spiritual being. God knows that, left completely to our own devices without regular reminders of our spiritual needs, many would degenerate into the preoccupation of satisfying earthly desires and appetites. This need for physical, mental, and spiritual regeneration is met in large measure by faithful observance of the Sabbath day.

"The third reason may be the most important of the three. It has to do with obedience to commandments as an expression of our love for God. Blessed are those who need no reasons other than their love for the Savior to keep his commandments. The response of Adam to the angel who asked Adam why he made a sacrifice unto the Lord is a model for all. Responded Adam, "I know not, save the Lord commanded me." (Moses 5:6)

Sometimes blessings aren't immediate, but we are promised joy and that all things will eventually work together for our good

(D&C 98:3). There is great peace in knowing you are doing what the Lord requires. Blessings will come. The Lord has said that "there is a law, irrevocably decreed in heaven before the foundations of this world, upon which all blessings are predicated—

"And when we obtain any blessing from God, it is by obedience to that law upon which it is predicated." (D&C 130:20-21)

The Law

The Bible is full of examples of what the Israelites could NOT do on the Sabbath and today we often think of Sunday in those terms as well. As a mother of four very active boys I'm often asked (every seven days to be exact), "What CAN we do on the Sabbath Day and still keep it holy?" They often grumble and complain that there isn't anything "good" to do on Sunday. I wrote this book to prove them wrong and to show them that there is plenty of "good" stuff to do! Part of my routine lecture to them on obeying commandment number four includes reminding them that Sunday should FEEL different than any of the other days of the week.

As members of the Church of Jesus Christ of Latter-day Saints we should understand the difference between the letter of the law and the spirit of the law. We often wish a prophet would just give us a specific list of do's and don'ts to refer to when deciding if we are keeping the Sabbath Day holy or not. When Joseph Smith was asked how he governed his people so well, he replied "I teach them correct principles and they govern themselves." (Journal of Discourses 10:57)

There is no absolute list of do's and don'ts for correct Sabbath observance, but the Lord has given us a good set of guidelines in Doctrine and Covenants 59:9-19. He teaches us that Sunday is a day to:

- Rest
- Worship
- Offer up vows in righteousness
- Confess our sins
- Partake of the sacrament
- Prepare food with singleness of heart
- Perfect our fasting

Rest From Our Labors

The Sabbath provides us with rest from our labors for both our mind and our body. It also provides us a weekly opportunity to worship, give meaningful service, and reflect on our past week's activities while preparing spiritually for our upcoming week. Active members of the Church often find Sundays to be exhausting, full of leadership meetings, Church services, firesides, compassionate service projects, teaching, interviews, and more. A careful balance of these things is important to keep the Sabbath Day holy.

Robert J. Matthews explained that "rest does not mean idleness; it signifies rather a change of emphasis. In plain terms, "keeping the Sabbath Day holy" means to cease or to rest from the secular labors of the week and to use the specified day in worshiping God and doing good to our fellow beings. It is a day for spiritual works and refreshment as compared to the secular accomplishments of other days." ("I Have a Question," *Ensign*, July 1978, p. 7) It is a day we give to the Lord.

Over ninety years ago the following item from the *Daily News* appeared in the *Liahona* under the caption "The Day of Rest":

"One of the facts upon which all men are agreed, whatever may be their view in life, is the need of a frequently recurring season of spiritual and physical refreshment. The life which was an unending vista of dusty days in the city would be a life from which we should all turn in despair. The hum of the wheels would drive the world mad. The soul would perish under the strain of material things and the body would perish with it. There is, therefore, no question of can't in the desire to keep our Sunday: it is a supreme necessity, and never more supreme than in these days, when the pace of life is always being quickened and men are becoming more and more like the parts of a giant machine whose operations they do not understand and whose roar dulls the mind." (Vol. 7, p. 445.)

True Worship

Why do we worship? The first of the Ten Commandments requires that men worship the Lord; the fourth commandment designates a day when it should be done with reverence and holiness. When the Lord created men and placed them on earth, he gave "commandments that they should love and serve him, the only living and true God, and that he should be the only being whom they should worship." (D&C 20:19)

God placed within man an instinctive desire to worship, to love and serve a power or being greater than ourselves. Some people say they can worship better out in nature than in a formal chapel. The question is, do they? There are untold blessings we receive when we worship together, as well as alone. A loving Father in Heaven has given us a place and time to gather together so that we can receive spiritual strength from one another.

President Brigham Young explained why the Lord wants us to set aside time to worship: "To keep us in remembrance of our God and our holy religion. ... We are so liable to forget—so prone to wander, that we need to have the Gospel sounded in our

ears as much as once, twice, or thrice a week, or, behold, we will
turn again to our idols." (*Discourses of Brigham Young*, sel. John A.
Widtsoe, 1978, p. 165)

President Spencer W. Kimball said: "We do not go to Sabbath
meetings to be entertained or even solely to be instructed. We go
to worship the Lord. It is an individual responsibility, and regard-
less of what is said from the pulpit, if one wishes to worship the
Lord in spirit and in truth, he may do so by attending his meetings, partaking of the sacrament, and contemplating the beauties
of the gospel. If the service is a failure to you, you have failed. No
one can worship for you; you must do your own waiting upon
the Lord." (*Teachings of Spencer W. Kimball*, ed. 1982, p. 515)

When we worship God we reveal our feelings about Him and
demonstrate our devotion and commitment. We can show worship through music, prayer, service, word, and reverence.

In addition to worship, President Kimball taught how we
might also observe the Sabbath: "The Sabbath is a day on which
to take inventory—to analyze our weaknesses, to confess our sins
to our associates and our Lord. It is a day on which to fast in
'sackcloth and ashes.' It is a day on which to read good books, a
day to contemplate and ponder ... a day to study the scriptures

and to prepare sermons, a day to nap and rest and relax, a day to visit the sick, a day to preach the gospel, a day to proselyte, a day to visit quietly with the family and get acquainted with our children, a day for proper courting, a day to do good, a day to drink at the fountain of knowledge and of instruction, a day to seek forgiveness of our sins, a day for the enrichment of our spirit and our soul, a day to restore us to our spiritual stature, a day to partake of the emblems of his sacrifice and atonement, a day to contemplate the glories of the gospel and of the eternal realms, a day to climb high on the upward path toward our Heavenly Father." (*Teachings*, p. 216)

The Sabbath

Today we observe the Sabbath on Sunday because Jesus was resurrected on Sunday. (Acts 20:7, 1 Corinthians 16:2) After the death and resurrection of Christ, the Lord's day became the first day of the week. President George Q. Cannon explained, "The Lord's day is the day on which He rose from the dead and on which His disciples at that period assembled to worship and break bread in His name. That was the first day of the week (John 20:1, Acts 20:7), as they counted time. This custom was observed in the primitive Christian Church." (Hoyt W. Brewster, Jr. *Doctrine and Covenants Encyclopedia*, 1988, p. 330) As Jesus came to life anew, we begin a new week, starting with reflection and gratitude on Sunday.

Mentioned more than two hundred times in the Old Testament alone, the word Sabbath comes from the Hebrew "shabbath," which means "to break off," "to desist," or "to rest." (*Encyclopedia of Mormonism*, 4 vols., 1992, 3:1241) Flavius Josephus, a religious scholar who lived during the first century after Jesus, stated that the Sabbath was a day "set apart from our labour (and) dedicated to the learning of our customs and laws" so that people might learn a good thing and avoid sin. (*The Complete Works of Josephus*, William Whiston, 1987, p. 338)

At the time of Christ, Jewish rabbis stressed two main themes in Sabbath observance. First, it was to be a day of rest. All work, agricultural, industrial, and domestic was forbidden unless it was in a particular instance necessary. In other words, if it could not be done the day before or put off until the day following without serious consequences.

The second major guideline was that the Sabbath was to be a day when everyone would be joyful, and eating luxuriously was one way they were joyous. Because of this, except for serious perils, fasting was not to be done on the Sabbath. The law also excluded mourning for the dead on the Sabbath. Visiting the sick was discouraged, but if done the visitor might say, "It is the Sabbath, one must not complain; you will soon be cured." (George Foot Moore, *Judaism*, 3 vols. Harvard University Press 1927, 2:37)

The Letter of the Law

What had once been a holy and sacred law, which stood as a sign identifying the Lord's peculiar people, had become a list of rabbinical rules which specified particular "do's" and "don'ts." A few of these Sabbath day rules and regulations were:

Certain kinds of knots were not to be tied or untied. It was all right to untie a knot that could be undone with one hand.

A fire was not to be started or extinguished.

One who was buried under ruins on the Sabbath, might be dug for and taken out, if alive, but if dead, he was to be left where he was until the Sabbath was over.

Unless death threatened, sickness was no excuse for violating rabbinical rules. Setting broken bones or putting back a dislocated joint was forbidden.

Travel was restricted to a distance slightly longer than a mile. This distance, which became known as "a Sabbath day's journey," was decided by measuring the distance from the tabernacle used during Moses' time to the tents of the furthermost camp and back again. If a person traveled farther than this distance, he was working and was therefore under sin.

Climbing trees, riding on an animal, swimming, clapping hands, and dancing were also prohibited.

The Spirit of the Law

Jesus Christ reinforced the importance of Sabbath observance during his ministry, however he also offered an enlightened understanding to followers by teaching them the spirit of the law. In the scriptures we read that Jesus spent his Sabbath days healing the sick, blessing the obedient, visiting the afflicted, reading scripture, and showing that it was "lawful to do good." Rather than drown in strict details and technicalities of law, the Lord showed us how we are to bless others and how we will be blessed by our Sabbath observance. When the Pharisees questioned the Savior about some of the things he did on the Sabbath, Jesus stated, "The Sabbath was made for man, and not man for the Sabbath." (Mark 2:27)

What is worthy or unworthy to do on the Sabbath day will have to be judged by each of us by trying to be honest with the Lord. After all, it is a test by which the Lord seeks to "prove you in all things" to see if your devotion is complete. (D&C 98:14) The key to keeping the Sabbath properly, like the key to obeying other gospel principles, is found in our hearts.

Modern prophets have not given us an exclusive list of things we should or should not do on the Sabbath, but they have directed us to scriptures that serve as guidelines. Many of those scriptures are listed in this book, but there are many more stories in the scriptures that teach the principle of obedience that can be applied to our attitude of Sabbath observance. The prophet Isaiah gave us a wonderful guideline for keeping the Sabbath day holy: "Turn away thy foot from ... doing thy pleasure on my holy day; and call the Sabbath a delight, the holy of the Lord, honourable; and ... honour him, not doing thine own ways, nor finding thine own pleasure, nor speaking thine own words" (Isaiah 58:13). A key to determine the appropriateness of Sabbath activities is to examine honestly their impact upon our spirituality.

A Sabbath Prepared

One way to more effectively keep the Sabbath day holy is to organize and prepare our homes and families in advance. Primary children sing a song which teaches that Saturday is a day to undertake certain chores so that they can be avoided on the Sabbath. If we think ahead we will buy our groceries, fill up our gas tanks, and complete other necessary tasks on other days of the week, leaving the Sabbath day to rest from our labors. A simple song and a simple principle, but it sends an important message to our Father in heaven that "we do always remember Him."

Saturday is a special day.
It's the day we get ready for Sunday:
We clean the house, and we shop at the store,
So we won't have to work until Monday.
We brush our clothes, and we shine our shoes,
And we call it our get-the-work-done day.
Then we trim our nails, and we shampoo our hair,
So we can be ready for Sunday!
(*Children's Songbook*, p. 196)

While it may be possible for an individual to have a restful Sabbath day filled with quiet reflection and thoughtful service, it requires a lot more preparation when children are in the home! Many families spend their time on Sundays searching for lost Church shoes and scriptures, and then race around from meeting to meeting throughout the day, praying their car will continue to function on gas fumes since no one bothered to fill the tank the day before. Families need to spend a little bit more time coordinating tasks before Sunday, perhaps during Family Council or Family Home Evening. The question could be raised "What can we do this week to prepare for a better Sabbath Day?"

President Spencer W. Kimball explained "Sabbath" observance is characterized as a matter of sacrifice and self-denial, but it is not so. It is merely a matter of scheduling and choosing seasons. There is time enough, particularly in our era of the world's history, during the six days of the week in which to do our work and play. Much can be done to organize and encourage weekday activities, avoiding the Sabbath." (*Tambuli*, July 1978, 1)

President Spencer W. Kimball also counseled students when he said "I hope students will use the Sabbath for studying only as an emergency. ... I believe that generally, with careful organization of time through the week, most studying can be done on weekdays, leaving the Sabbath for worship. There might be times when one would feel forced to study, when he might feel that it was an ox in the mire. I am expressing only my personal opinions on this matter, but since we are talking to students, it would be my hope that your studying could be done in the season thereof and not as a cramming process just before you go on Monday mornings." (*Teachings*, pp. 227-229)

On February 1, 1980, when the First Presidency announced the consolidated Sunday meeting schedule, the following counsel was given: "A greater responsibility will be placed upon the individual members and families for properly observing the Sabbath day. More time will be available for personal study of the scriptures and family-centered gospel study.

"Other appropriate Sabbath activities, such as strengthening family ties, visiting the sick and the homebound, giving service to others, writing personal and family histories, genealogical work, and missionary work, should be planned and carried out.

"It is expected that this new schedule of meetings and activities will result in greater spiritual growth for members of the Church." (*Church News*, 2 Feb. 1980, p. 3)

The Plan

Four young boys aren't going to sit and read scriptures all day long. Well, at least mine aren't! While this book makes an attempt to explain what it means to truly "worship" the Savior, it also offers practical ideas on HOW to worship and praise God on Sunday and actually have your family enjoy it! This is not a book of CAN'TS, but rather a brainstorm of things you CAN do that are in keeping with the spirit of the Lord's hallowed day.

Included in this book, along with suggested ideas, are quotes from prophets, General Authorities and others to help us catch the spirit of the Lord's special day. In order to receive the spiritual strength the Lord had planned for Sabbath observance, we cannot passively spend the day, but instead, we need to be actively involved. Sunday is the Lord's day, a day to do His work.

In this book there are more than 350 suggestions that will maybe even inspire you to create more ideas you can try with your family. Every family is unique, but the goal of Sabbath observance is the same: to honor the Savior on His special day, worship and glorify Him, and keep His day holy. We have been promised by prophets both ancient and modern that as we keep his commandments we will be blessed abundantly.

The ideas in the book can be used individually or as families. You may need to adjust some of the ideas to fit your own situation. You may want to have everyone in your family take turns picking out several activities each week or assign one person to be responsible for an entire month's worth of Sundays. You could set a goal to try each idea in the book, placing a checkmark next to each completed activity, before you can repeat any of them. Another idea would be to gather all of the ideas by theme for a music Sabbath, or Missionary Sunday, for example.

It would be fun to keep a Sabbath journal and record what you and your family do each Sunday and the feelings and spiritual experiences that are created by participating in some of these suggested activities. You won't even hurt my feelings if you cut up the ideas from the pages of this book into slips of paper and randomly draw out ideas from a hat each Sunday! Perhaps you will want to reserve some of these activities to be done ONLY on Sundays so the children will eagerly anticipate them each week.

Sunday should especially be a day when our families feel love for one another and for our Father in heaven. We do not have to fill every moment of the day with activities for our children, but rather, allow them to have some quiet time to reflect and feel peaceful refreshment. Such quiet time will help them learn to hear the spirit. If we are engaged in too many busy activities we won't be able to hear the "still small voice." Hopefully these ideas will be a catalyst to help you think of more ways to sincerely worship the Lord on his holy day. Sunday can truly be a day of spiritual celebration!

I'd like to share one final thought with you about why the Lord gave us a Sabbath Day. Because Heavenly Father is so wise and loving, He offers us countless opportunities to learn about our Savior and Redeemer, that we may become more like Him. When we study the scriptures we need to remember that they point us to Jesus Christ and that all things in the gospel are symbols of Christ in some way. The Sabbath Day is a day of rest, a day built into our very lives to remind us that, ultimately it is Jesus Christ who will give us rest! He told us "Come unto me, all ye that are heavy laden and I will give you rest." (Matthew 11:28-29). We are also told that "the Lord's rest is the fullness of his glory." (D&C 84:24) May God bless you with an abundance of His spirit as you strive to draw closer to Him on His holy day!

Ideas for the Sabbath

IDEAS

- Wear your Sunday clothes all day to help you remember how to behave in accordance with the Sabbath.

- Ask yourself, "What would the Savior do today?"

- Make a list of activities you could eliminate from your usual Sabbath activities to make Sunday a more spiritual day.

- Have a monthly "Theme Sunday" such as Neighbor Sunday, Manners Sunday, Ancestor Sunday, Music Sunday, Church History Sunday, Pioneer Sunday, Grandparents Sunday, Church President Sunday, etc. Focus your Sunday activities and studies around that particular subject.

- Go to Church! Bring a friend!

- Attend Church meetings in a ward or branch where another language is spoken, such as Spanish or sign language.

- Attend any meetings that your Church calling requires, such as Ward Council, Welfare meeting, BYC, PPI, etc.

Arts & Crafts

IDEAS

- Make paper dolls to use with some scripture stories.

- Make your own flannel board figures of scripture stories.

- Make "Quiet Books" using photographs of your family members being reverent in different ways. Small children can look at the books during Sacrament meeting to remind them to be reverent.

- Make gifts for people you home teach, visit teach or would just like to lift up when they're feeling down. Use and develop your creative talents.

- Make a collage or draw pictures showing your blessings.

- Draw a picture of your family.

- Draw a self-portrait of how you look now and the person you want to become.

- Learn how to knit or crochet. Find an older sister to teach you.

―――――――――――――――――――

"Sunday being the Lord's Day, it is a day on which men should do the Lord's work, and do it exclusively. There should be no unnecessary work of a temporal nature, no recreation, no unnecessary travel, no joy riding, and the like. The Sabbath is a day for affirmative spiritual worship."

—Bruce R. McConkie
Mormon Doctrine, 2nd ed. 1966, pp. 658-59

―――――――――――――――――――

IDEAS

- Make charts for family members to show their progress in scripture reading or memorizing certain passages.

- Have young children make a scrapbook or collage of "Things we can do on Sunday." Pictures could be taken from old Church magazines or drawings that the children make themselves.

- Make puzzles out of pictures from old Church magazines.

- Make play dough and create people and shapes from favorite scripture stories such as a Liahona, the gold plates or Noah's ark.

- Make a special bookmark for your scripture reading.

- Make a "Sunday Only" box and fill it with Sunday projects, books, tapes, etc. Only get it out on the Sabbath.

- Make a birthday card for the Prophet. Find out when his birthday is!

"People frequently wonder where to draw the line; what is worthy and what is unworthy to do upon the Sabbath. But if one loves the Lord with all his heart, might, mind and strength; if one can put away selfishness and curb desire; if one can measure each Sabbath activity by the yardstick of worshipfulness; if one is honest with his Lord and with himself; if one offers a 'broken heart and contrite spirit,' it is quite unlikely that there will be Sabbath breaking in that person's life."

—President Spencer W. Kimball
The Teachings of Spencer W. Kimball, 1982, p. 219

IDEAS

- Create a family mailbox to keep inside your home that you fill with sweet letters to each other.

- Start working on a quilt for a baby, college student or new bride.

- Start gathering scraps of old favorite clothing and fabric to create a memory quilt or pillow.

- Tape record yourself or your children reading a story from the scriptures. Draw pictures to go with it. Keep it to enjoy over and over again or share it with someone who can't read or is losing his or her vision.

- Make a gift or treat for your home teachers for the next time they come.

- Make a gift or treat for your Bishop or other church leaders who bless your lives.

- Create a family flag or banner to display in your home.

"Our observance or nonobservance of the Sabbath is an unerring measure of our attitude toward the Lord personally and toward his suffering in Gethsemane, his death on the cross, and his resurrection from the dead. It is a sign of whether we are Christians in very deed, or whether our conversion is so shallow that commemoration of his atoning sacrifice means little or nothing to us."

—Elder Mark E. Peterson
Ensign, May 1975, p. 49

IDEAS

- Design and create costumes to wear while telling a scripture story at your next Family Home Evening.

- Make puppets or paper dolls of each member in your family. Role play different scenarios.

- Create special awards and certificates to be given to family members for accomplishing certain tasks or behaviors.

- Have your children begin planning what they will create to enter the national "Reflections" contest held every year. Find out what the theme is.

President George Albert Smith explained what our attitude toward the Sabbath should be: "[The Lord] has set apart one day in seven, not to make it a burden, but to bring joy into our lives and cause that our homes may be the gathering place of the family, ... increasing our love for one another."

"Obey the Commandments," *Improvement Era*, Jan. 1949, p. 9

IDEAS

- Recreate Solomon's temple, Laban's sword, Moses' tablets or some other church artifact out of craft supplies.

- Make homemade cards for any upcoming birthdays, anniversaries, or when you just want to say "thinking of you" or "get well."

- Create an alphabet book using pictures of your family holding various objects or doing certain things that start with each letter. Use gospel-oriented words for each alphabet letter, such as Apostle, Book of Mormon, Commandment, Disciple, etc.

- Think about what gift from the heart you could give to your parents on the next Mother's Day or Father's Day.

- Draw cartoon strips of the scriptures.

- Do shadow drawings using a lamp and paper to draw the profiles of everyone in the family.

"I often wonder what happened to the good old saying, 'Sunday best.' If our dress deteriorates to everyday attire, our actions seem to follow the type of clothing we wear. "Of course, we would not expect our children to remain dressed in their church clothes all day, but neither would we expect them to dress in clothes that would not be appropriate for the Sabbath."

—Elder L. Tom Perry
Ensign, November 1984, p. 19

IDEAS

- Dip the children's hands in washable paint and have them put their handprints on a paper to keep in their scrapbooks.

- Create costumes and props and take family photos of you portraying characters from the scriptures.

- Make an "armor of God" costume and talk about the symbolism.

- Make special boxes, jars, or containers for tithing and missionary funds for children to use. Decorate them with gospel pictures you draw or cut out of old church magazines.

- Start thinking about what gifts you could make or create for next Christmas without spending money, but rather come from your heart instead.

- Decorate a pillow case with scriptures or other sweet thoughts to fill your mind as you drift off to sleep.

Cooking

IDEAS

- Try a new recipe. Have your family look through recipe books and pick out something they've never tried before. Remember to keep it simple.

- Teach the kids how to cook something simple.

- Plan a weekly menu. Have each family select a meal they could help cook.

- Make treats to take to Seminary tomorrow.

- Have a pioneer meal. Eat outside around a fire, if possible. Sing pioneer songs and share their inspiring stories. Put cream in baby food jars to shake while you're telling the stories, turning the cream into butter.

- Learn about the traditions and foods eaten during Passover. Find out if there is a special Passover event nearby where you could attend as a guest.

- Bake cookies to give away to friends and neighbors.

"God has commanded us to care for the spirit, as well as for the body, and give it food in due season, and He set aside the Sabbath day that man might rest from his temporal labors and go to the house of the Lord and be fed with that holy influence which nourishes the spirit of man. That is why we meet together on the Sabbath day. Our spirits need their food, the same as do our bodies and if we neglect them, they will starve and dwindle and die upon the same principle that the body will die when deprived of its proper nourishment."

—Elder Orson F. Whitney
"The Day of Rest,"
Liahona—The Elders' Journal, vol. 7, p. 530

IDEAS

- Organize your recipes. Plan a special section for Sunday meals that are simple and don't require too much time.

- Pull out that crock pot and use it to cut down on cooking time in the kitchen. Fill it up with ingredients before you leave for Church and by the time you get back it should be ready! Try new simple recipes.

- Rediscover the fun of cooking outdoors. Use your barbeque or grill again.

- Have the children create a new recipe using ingredients around the kitchen.

- In order to prepare food "with singleness of heart" (D&C 59:13) plan a simple dinner of cold cuts, cheese, crackers, fruit and vegetables.

Culture

IDEAS

- Learn about other cultures. Find out how the Church is progressing in different parts of the world.

- Find a pen pal you could write to who is a member of the Church somewhere else in the world.

- Find out if there is a local book club you could join or start one yourself. Choose uplifting literature and classics to study.

- Listen to classical music. Learn about some of the famous composers.

- Study famous works of art. Learn about some of the famous artists in history.

- Read good poetry and then try to write some!

- Plan a special family home evening or family dinner about a certain country. Learn about the food, clothing, traditions and culture. Find someone from that country to invite over to share your evening!

"A man who considers his religion a slavery has not begun to comprehend the real nature of religion. To such men, religion is a life of crosses and mortifications. They find their duty unpleasant and onerous. It is to them a law of restraint and constraint. They are constantly oppressed with what they denominate a 'sense of duty.' Are they happy in that condition? I say no; only those are happy who are doing their duty."

—J. Golden Kimball

IDEAS

- Have everyone in the family choose different books to read during the next few Sundays. When everyone has finished reading have each person present an oral report about what they learned from their book.

- Find out what upcoming events there are in your community that you could attend that would be virtuous, lovely, or of good report, or praiseworthy.

- Start a reading contest with your family. Choose a time frame and see how many pages each person can read with a prize for the winner.

- Check your local library and schools to see what cultural events are being offered that you could attend.

Emergency Preparedness

IDEAS

- Do an inventory of your food storage. Make a list of things you could do to improve your emergency preparedness. Talk with other families you know who seem to be well prepared and get ideas from them.

- Organize your ward or branch to collect items to provide a 72-hour kit for the missionaries serving in your Church unit.

- Update the emergency preparedness bags in your cars. Refresh the food and batteries.

- Update all of your smoke alarm batteries and review your emergency plans of exit with your family. Prepare "every needful thing."

"May I take you back 142 years when there was, of course, no tabernacle here, nor temple, nor Temple Square. On July 24, 1847, the pioneer company of our people came into this valley. An advance group had arrived a day or two earlier. Brigham Young arrived on Saturday. The next day, Sabbath services were held both in the morning and in the afternoon. There was no hall of any kind in which to meet. I suppose that in the blistering heat of that July Sunday they sat on the tongues of their wagons and leaned against the wheels while the Brethren spoke. The season was late, and they were faced with a gargantuan and immediate task if they were to grow seed for the next season. But President Young pleaded with them not to violate the Sabbath then or in the future."

—President Gordon B. Hinckley

Ensign, Nov. 1989, p. 51

IDEAS

- Choose a special family code word for your family to use on certain emergency situations such as when someone else needs to pick up your child from school when you are unable. The password is given to ensure the child that another adult has permission. Do role plays of scenarios that teach your children to be safe.

- Sign up for classes in first aid and CPR. They are offered at local fire stations, churches and community colleges.

- Hold a fire drill in your home. Discuss how you can make your home more safe.

- Help your son work towards eaerning his Boy Scout first aid merit badge or Cub Scout safety requirements.

Family Home Evening

IDEAS

- Make a family home evening packet to give to another family.

- Prepare tomorrow's family home evening lesson.

- Create an object lesson you could use during Family Home Evening or in another class you teach at church.

- Make a puppet show about a scripture story, then share it at Family Home Evening or even at Primary.

- Make a crossword puzzle about a scripture story or parable.

- Cut out pictures as visual aids from the *Friend* magazine to use for future Family Home Evenings.

- Make your own illustrations to stories that teach gospel principles. Share them during Family Home Evening or draw them in your scriptures near the appropriate passages.

- Find out what the Primary, Young Men/Young Women themes are for the year and incorporate them into your future Family Home Evenings or activities.

"What are the consequences of disobedience in keeping the Sabbath day holy? Our spiritual natures, needing spiritual food, shrink and die without it. Physical deterioration also results. Let us, therefore, in the midst of our worldly callings and associations, not forget that paramount duty which we owe to ourselves and to our God."

—President Joseph F. Smith
Juvenile Instructor, March 1912, p. 145

IDEAS

- Plan a special Spotlight night for a family member to be done at dinner time or Family Home Evening.

- Invite someone over to share Family Home Evening with you on Monday night. Make a phone call or design a special invitation. Your guest could include non-members or even another family in the ward whom you would like to get to know better.

- Organize a group of mothers who want to create a Family Home Evening group who will make and share visual aids for their Monday night lessons.

- Create a special Family Home Evening bag where you will put one item in it from each week's lesson. After a month or two pull out the items one at a time and review the lessons you shared.

- Create a special poster or chart to help your family keep track of whose turn it is to teach the next Family Home Evening lesson, prepare the refreshments, offer prayers, etc.

Family Time

IDEAS

- Write to grandparents, aunts, uncles or cousins and share photos of what you've been doing lately.

- Have a "companion interview" with your spouse.

- Hold a family council.

- Have individual interviews with your children. Review their goals, hopes and dreams.

- Plan the next week's events with personal goals in mind. Organize your personal and family calendar.

- Go through the Boy Scout Handbook and pick out some projects to work on with your son.

- Go through the Young Woman's manual and pick out some goals to work on with your daughter. Review her progress on her Young Womanhood Achievement award and Faith in God booklet.

- Take family photos outside somewhere in a beautiful setting.

"The Lord's day was, of course, Sunday, and on this day the Latter-day Saints have been commanded to observe the weekly Sabbath. So far as the Latter-day Saints are concerned, the Lord has spoken. This settles the question."

—Joseph Fielding Smith
Answers to Gospel Questions, vol.2, p. 59

IDEAS

- Write a list of all the good qualities of each family member. Share the list with them or just refer to it when you're having a hard time remembering why you really do love them!

- Think about what family picture you'd like to take and use to send with your Christmas cards next year.

- Ask your mom or dad to tell you about when they were little.

- Make a cassette recording of your children's laughter. Have children tell jokes or share stories about funny things you have done as a family.

- Show home movies or slides of when everyone was younger. Tell stories of when parents were young and how they met, what things were like then, etc.

- Tape record or video the family sharing their testimonies to play back on a Sunday a year from now.

"I wish I had the power to convert this whole Church to the observance of the Sabbath. I know our people would be more richly blessed of the Lord if they would walk in faithfulness in the observance of the Sabbath."

—President Gordon B. Hinkley
Heber City/Springville Utah regional conference,
Priesthood leadership meeting, 13 May 1995

IDEAS

- Read a story to a child. Even better, read two!

- Plan your next family vacation. Talk about how you will keep the Sabbath Day holy if your trip involves a Sunday stay.

- Update your family movies and turn them into DVDs.

- Plan a "Daddy/Daughter" date or "Me & Mom" date.

- Think up some new family traditions you want to start incorporating in your life.

- Visit relatives.

- Plan a family reunion. Research locations where you could gather for the big event. Write or call relatives who could help you organize it. Make assignments. Pick a theme.

- Create a family web site with photos so your friends and relatives can see what you've been doing and how the children have grown.

"When we or our children are faced with the decision of whether or not an activity is appropriate for the Sabbath, we might ask ourselves: Is it honoring the Lord? Is it doing good? Is it spiritually uplifting? Would Jesus approve of it? Following such guidelines can turn the Sabbath into a delight."

—*Church Handbook for Families*

IDEAS

- Start a family Round Robin newsletter. Write about the activities and accomplishments of your family and then send it on to another relative who adds information about his. Each family adds to the letter and sends it on until it gets back to the beginning, when you update your family's information and start over. Letters can be kept in a special family binder.

- Cuddle on the couch with your child.

- Make a sign to hang in your home that uses each letter of your family's last name to create a mission statement. For example:

    S – Stand for truth and righteousness

    M – Missionary Work

    I – Integrity

    T – Temple Worthiness

    H – Honor Covenants

- Call your parents!

"The Sabbath spirit is the spirit of helping, loving, lifting, and teaching family, friends, and neighbors. It is a day of opportunities to lose ourselves in the service of others. It is a day for repenting, for giving up such things as evil speaking, hard feelings, sinful habits, unkindness, pettiness, meanness, uncharitable attitudes and actions, pride and irreverence."

—Dean M. Hansen

"I Have A Question," *Ensign*, June 1995, p. 66

IDEAS

- Go through your family's Church clothes to see if everything is in order. Do shoes fit? Are clothes mended? Are ties cleaned? Plan a week day when everyone can help prepare them for Sunday.

- Create family committees that each person can be "Chairman" over such as "Social Director, Family Home Evening Chairman, Service Coordinator, Time Management Tsar, Family Historian, etc. Have each person report on committee efforts at each month's Family Council.

- Have a family testimony meeting.

- Start a special "funny book" where you record all of the funny things each of the children say.

Friends

IDEAS

- Invite a friend over to play this week.

- E-mail someone you'd like to keep in touch with.

- Meet some of your neighbors. If they're new bring them a copy of the local newspaper or list of helpful phone numbers, along with a plate of cookies and your phone number. If you're the ones who are new introduce your family with a plate of goodies.

- Invite two or three families from Church to your home for ice cream "Sundays" and talk about your favorite Sunday traditions.

- Find a way to fellowship less active members.

- Adopt the newest family or member of the ward and help them get to know others.

- Look up old friends who have moved away and try to reconnect with them.

"If Christ be the example of proper Sabbath observance, then we note with some interest that his Sabbaths were spent preaching in the synagogues, teaching in the temple, and healing the sick."

—Joseph Fielding McConkie

IDEAS

- Organize a neighborhood party you could have on another day so people can get to know each other better.

- Make a list of friends you could invite to attend this month's Enrichment Night. Be brave and call them!

- Arrange play dates for your children for the upcoming week.

- Leave treats at the doorstep of two families in the ward with a note telling them to carry on the good deed. Within a few weeks most of the ward will have received a fun surprise!

Games

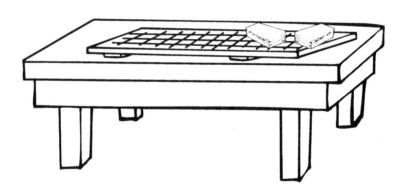

IDEAS

- Create a gospel version of your favorite board game by substituting the original questions with gospel questions. Be creative and make temple markers or choose prizes that represent blessings.

- Make "Concentration" games using pictures you draw yourself of gospel-centered ideas. Make two cards of each picture and place them face down. Players take turns trying to match up the two cards.

- Play Charades using scripture stories, names of prophets or other Church events.

- Make flash cards to memorize the Articles of Faith, scriptures, faces of General Authorities or something else you want to memorize about the gospel.

- Make your own playing cards out of pictures of gospel principles you cut out of old Church magazines or that you draw yourself.

"This, then, is the heart of the matter. The Sabbath was made for our good—not to enslave the spirit, but to feed it. And when the spirit is fed, the Sabbath day becomes the remarkable blessing that the Lord intended it to be."

—Russell C. Harris
"Questions and Answers," *New Era*, Nov. 1971, p. 6

- Have a Scripture Chase event! Use scriptures that your family already knows or is working on or use the selected scriptures from Seminary.

- Create matching games for toddlers using pictures of temples or drawings from Church magazines. Cut the pictures in half and the children have to match up the two sides.

- Create several stations around the house where different Sunday activities take place such as listening to the scriptures on tape, reading Church magazines, writing letters to missionaries, drawing pictures for grandparents, etc. Use a timer and have the family rotate through the stations every 15 minutes or so.

- Play relationship-building games with your family, like the ones they do at youth conferences and family retreats.

- Make dot-to-dot pictures of gospel themes such as the nativity scene or the stripling warriors.

"In our Christian world in many places we still have business establishments open for business on the sacred Sabbath. We are sure the cure of this lies in ourselves, the buying public. Certainly the stores and business houses would not remain open if we, the people, failed to purchase from them. Will you all please reconsider this matter. Take it to your home evenings and discuss it with your children. It would be wonderful if every family determined that henceforth no Sabbath purchase would be made."

—President Spencer W. Kimball
"The Time to Labor Is Now," *Ensign*, Nov. 1975, p. 4

IDEAS

- Create a treasure hunt using scriptures as clues. Choose an object to hunt for such as a new set of scriptures, church stickers or a favorite dessert.

- Play "Family Spin the Bottle." The family sits in a circle and spins a soda pop bottle. Someone spins the bottle on the floor, then tells what he or she likes about the person to whom it points. Next, that person spins the bottle and the process is repeated.

- Make new chess pieces out of clay for your chess board using characters from the scriptures.

- Do the crossword puzzles and games from the *Friend* magazine.

Genealogy

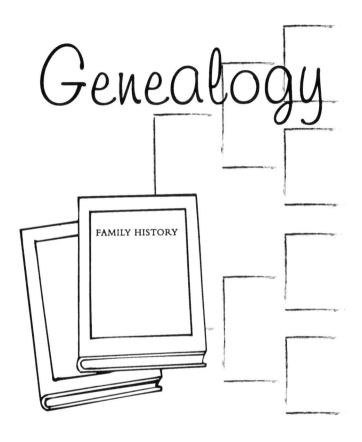

FAMILY HISTORY

IDEAS

- Do genealogy name extraction. Ask your Ward's Family History consultant how you can help. He or she will be happy to teach you how to do it.

- Start writing your autobiography or update it, detailing your spiritual experiences.

- Update family photos and scrapbooks.

- Plan a scrapbook party when friends can come over and work on their photo pages together.

- Like Nephi did with the small plates, keep a special journal where you record only your spiritual experiences.

- Check out some genealogy web sites.

- Find out when the next genealogy seminar or class is occurring in your community so you can learn more. Find out what resources your area has.

"This day...is called the Sabbath, from the Hebrew shabbath meaning day of rest. The rest, though important, is incidental to the true keeping of the Sabbath. What is more important is that the Sabbath is an holy day—a day of worship, one in which men turn their whole souls to the Lord, renew their covenants with him, and feed their souls upon the things of the Spirit."

—Bruce R. McConkie

Mormon Doctrine, 2nd ed, 1966, pp. 658-659

IDEAS

- Learn how to use the latest version of the Church's Personal Ancestral File (PAF) software. Then update your genealogy records onto the computer.

- Make a cassette recording of your grandparents sharing their memories. Be sure to record their laughter!

- Help children make a scrapbook of their favorite papers from school. Label and date each item. Write about what those projects taught and why they were so important.

- Teach your children how to fill out a pedigree chart, including their own name on the form.

- Tell stories about ancestors and learn more about them.

- Create a photo pedigree chart of your family.

- Research your family's historic coat of arms. Find out about the symbols.

"Questions regarding appropriate behavior on the Sabbath are easily resolved when you study [the] scriptures and then determine what sign you choose to give to God of your regard for him."

—Elder Russell M. Nelson

"Standards of the Lord's Standard-bearers,"

Ensign, Aug. 1991, p. 10

IDEAS

- Volunteer to take pictures of tombstones for counties. There are web sites on-line where you can send your photos so that other genealogists can benefit from your efforts.

- Visit a cemetery where one of your loved ones was laid to rest.

- Write down lessons you have learned from your parents. Keep them in a book to pass down to your children.

- Find out if you're related to any of the other people in your phone book with your same last name. Don't be shy—just start calling!

Goals

IDEAS

- Write a list of all of the people you'd like to meet during your life and what questions you would ask them if you met.

- Write a list of all the places you'd like to see in your lifetime. Research them and start making plans to make a trip to those sites really happen!

- Review your personal goals for the year and/or week. How are you doing on your New Year's resolutions?

- Write a letter to yourself to read in a year or even just a month. Talk about your hopes and dreams and what you plan on doing to make them come true.

- Make a "Future Scrapbook" using pictures of what you want to be or events you want to happen in the future (temple marriage, mission, family, etc.) Set goals to make them happen.

- Begin a list of all the things you want to accomplish during your lifetime.

"Strange as it may seem, some Latter-day Saints, faithful in all other respects, justify themselves in missing their church meetings on occasion for recreational purposes, feeling that the best fishing will be missed if one is not at the stream Sunday or that the vacation will not be long enough if one does not set off on Sunday or that one will miss a movie he wanted to see if he does not go on the Sabbath. And in their breach of the Sabbath they often take their families with them. The Savior said: "Whosoever therefore shall break one of these least commandments, and shall teach men so, he shall be called the least in kingdom of heaven." (Matthew 5:19)

—President Spencer W. Kimball
"The Sabbath—A Delight," *Tambuli*, July 1978, p. 1

IDEAS

- Create a notebook for each child where you record their goals, their finances (allowances), and school project deadlines. Go over the information each week informally or during a parent interview.

- Consider habits in your life that are making you just BE rather than BECOME. Identify a bad habit you can break and create a new good habit that will help you improve yourself this week.

- Begin a "Pursuit of Excellence" goal program to challenge yourself or use the Mother's Academy program offered by American Mothers, Inc.

- Check out colleges and universities that offer free improvement classes and sign up for one of them.

- Update your will and other legal documents. Make sure your "house is in order."

Journal Writing

IDEAS

- Record your thoughts in your journal about keeping the Sabbath Day holy.

- Start a gratitude journal. Each day record three things you are grateful for.

- Have everyone write in their journal for 15 minutes. Help younger children record their thoughts by dictating to older children who can then write their words down.

- Write your own epitaph. Think about how you want to be remembered and evaluate how your life is going so far.

- Create a jar or box with slips of paper that suggest various topics for you to write about in your journal.

Media

IDEAS

- Borrow videos, books, or even flannel board stories from the Church library. The ward library is one of the Church's best kept secrets. Be sure to return them!

- Watch some gospel-oriented videos. There are so many great ones out there now. Talk about what you learned or how you felt inspired by them.

- Listen to gospel-oriented cassette tapes. There are dramatized stories, speeches, as well as the scriptures simply being read on tape. Get a fire roaring in the fireplace or light some candles to create a fun atmosphere while you lounge around listening.

- Make your own video of scripture stories. Share videos with other families or even with a Seminary or Primary class.

- Watch BYUTV. If you don't have access to it, call or write to your cable or satellite company to request it.

- Listen to LDS radio. It's carried on some cable and satellite chanels and you can even find it on the Internet.

"And the matter of Sabbath observance remains to this day as one of the great tests which divides the righteous from the worldly and wicked."

—Bruce R. McConkie
Mormon Doctrine, 2nd ed. 1966, p. 658

IDEAS

- Find out what kind of web sites are on the Internet for members of the Church.

- Visit the BYU web site and find out what's happening with the Lord's University.

- Check out old filmstrips from the Church library to watch at home as a family. Have your family tell what is happening in each frame without listening to the accompanying cassette.

- Visit the Church's Distribution web site. You'll need to get your membership record number from your ward clerk in order to purchase on-line on another day.

- Go on the Internet and find out about upcoming Church conferences for families, women, and genealogy, such as "Know your Religion" and BYU Education Week. Start planning a trip to attend one of these great events!

- Watch broadcasts of BYU devotionals. You can often find copies of them in your ward library.

"The Lord has given the Sabbath day for your benefit and has commanded you to keep it holy. On this sacred, holy day, worship the Lord, strengthen family relationships, help others, and draw close to the Lord. Many activities are appropriate for the Sabbath; however, it is not a holiday. You should avoid seeking entertainment or spending money on this day."

—*For the Strength of Youth* pamphlet

IDEAS

- Check out some of the gospel-oriented software that include games, talks, and books written by members of the Church.

- Download the scriptures or hymns onto your handheld computer.

- Talk to friends about forming a "clean video club" where families could swap good videos.

Missionary

IDEAS

- Using a copy of the missionary discussions, mark your scriptures to use the color code system like the full-time missionaries do.

- Every Ward and Stake should have a posted list of missionary and service opportunities. Check out what you could do to help in your area.

- Invite a friend to attend church with you next Sunday.

- Write to missionaries who are serving from your ward.

- Call the Mission office nearest you and ask if there are some missionaries who haven't received mail or support from home that you could help.

- Pray for missionary opportunities. Try to identify a person or family you could share the gospel with next week.

"Keep the Sabbath day holy, set it aside as a day of rest, a day of meeting together to perform your sacraments and listen to the words of life, and thus be found keeping the commandments, and setting a good example before your children."

—John Taylor
The Gospel Kingdom,
sel. G. Homer Durham, 1943, p. 339

IDEAS

- Find out if your ward or branch missionaries need to pay for their pamphlets and copies of the Book of Mormon. Offer to get some for them by next week. Even write your testimony inside before you give them to the missionaries.

- Invite the missionaries over for dinner. Learn about who they have been teaching and find out how you can help.

- Invite the missionaries over to teach you a discussion. Even better, invite a non-member to listen with you!

- Teach your future missionaries how to sew on a button or mend torn clothes.

- Get a fresh supply of the Church's "Pass-along cards." Make a list of people you could share them with. Put some in your car, wallet, purse, or backpack so you'll be ready for a missionary moment at any time.

"I have a firm conviction that the greatest guarantee for success in business for a Latter-day Saint is to honor the Sabbath day as the Lord has commanded."

—Ezra Taft Benson
Ensign, May 1971, p. 7

IDEAS

- Make sack lunches for the missionaries that are being transferred and will be traveling all day.

- Volunteer to do exchanges with the missionaries in your ward.

- Learn the missionary discussions.

- Think about what you could do to "lengthen your stride" as a member missionary.

Music

I D E A S

- Listen to a new hymn or Primary song and learn the words.

- Practice musical instruments. Offer to provide a musical number in Sacrament meeting or even in a local nursing home or hospital.

- Create a family song.

- Play "Name that tune" with your family by humming the first notes of a hymn and seeing who can guess it. Then you can all sing the song together.

- Teach children how to lead music and take turns pretending to be the ward choir director.

- Learn to sing a church song using sign language.

- Learn about the background of a certain Church hymn or Primary song and then start memorizing the words. Practice the words and play the song during the upcoming week.

"The Sabbath is not just another day on which we merely rest from our work, free to spend it as our light-mindedness may suggest. It is a holy day, the Lord's Day, to be spent as a day of worship and reverence."

—The First Presidency message, 1959

IDEAS

- Draw pictures to go with some of the Church hymns or Primary songs. Offer to share them with the Primary chorister.

- Practice singing a song you could sing in Sacrament meeting as a special musical number. If you don't want to sing a solo, call others who could sing with you.

- Write a song about a gospel topic.

- Create your own songs to help memorize scripture verses.

- Learn how to play a new musical instrument. Find a teacher. Sign up for a class.

- Invite friends over to share each other's musical talents, then have a special musical evening.

- Learn to play a Sacrament hymn on an instrument.

- Write new words to a familiar hymn.

"It is true that some people must work on the Sabbath. And, in fact, some of the work that is truly necessary—caring for the sick, for example—may actually serve to hallow the Sabbath. However, in such activities our motives are an important consideration. When men and women are willing to work on the Sabbath to increase their wealth, they are breaking the commandments; for money taken in on the Sabbath, if the work is unnecessary, is unclean money."

—Spencer W. Kimball

"The Sabbath A Delight," *Tambuli*, July 1978, p. 1

IDEAS

- Learn to play a Church hymn on the piano. The Church distribution center has a great little keyboard and beginner's course you can buy very inexpensively.

- Go "Sunday caroling." Visit other members in your ward or branch and sing them a few hymns to lift their spirits.

- The Church hymn book and even the Primary songbook include scripture references for each musical selection. Make footnotes in your scriptures that show those connections.

Outdoors, Exercise, and God's Creations

IDEAS

- Take a walk. Thank Heavenly Father for giving us such a beautiful world to live in.

- Take a nap. Hang on a hammock outside and enjoy the fresh air.

- Take a walk with one child at a time and talk about whatever THEY want to talk about. No lecturing, just listening.

- Go on a picnic in a park. Enjoy the beautiful surroundings.

- Learn how to meditate.

- Learn relaxation techniques such as deep breathing with gentle stretches.

- Do science experiments to understand God's fascinating world. Study how the Lord used scientific principles in the scriptures.

- Grow different kinds of sprouts and try a new dish using them. Start using them in your salads, sandwiches, and meals for a healthier diet.

"The Sabbath contemplates quiet tranquility, peace of mind and spirit. It is a day to get rid of selfish interests and absorbing activities."

—Spencer W. Kimball
The Teachings of Spencer W. Kimball, 1982, p. 215

IDEAS

- Grow crystals and talk about how cool science is.

- Plan your vegetable garden. Plan how you could improve the beauty of your yard. Learn about different plants, shrubs, flowers, and trees. Save the actual yard work, however, for a different day of the week.

- Learn about composting. Plan a compost area that will fit the size and needs of your yard.

- Have a "vegetable swap" get-together, where gardening enthusiasts share extra fruit and veggies from their crops.

- Make potpourri from your flowers, pinecones, or other items from your yard.

- Make bookmarks, stationery or other gifts using pressed flowers from your yard or ones you have gathered on a nature walk.

Community Service

IDEAS

- Find out about some of the organizations that are trying to improve the moral quality of the media, such as www.onemillionmoms.com, www.conservativealerts.com, www.afa.net, www.grassfire.org and www.ccv.org. There are so many more great groups out there we can link up with to stand for truth and righteousness!

- Call 1–800-GIVE LIFE and find out when and where you can donate blood in your area.

- Volunteer to help at your local library.

- Teach someone to read. Improve literacy in your area.

- Find out how you can volunteer at your child's school with PTA or in his classroom.

- Choose a charity you can donate used items to. Find out if they'll come to your home for pick up or if you have to deliver items to them. Choose a day when your family can go through closets and drawers to find items to give away to charity.

"We urge all Latter-day Saints to set this holy day apart from activities of the world and consecrate themselves by entering into a spirit of worship, thanksgiving, service, and family-centered activities appropriate to the Sabbath. As Church members endeavor to make their Sabbath activities compatible with the intent and Spirit of the Lord, their lives will be filled with joy and peace."

—The First Presidency, 1993

I D E A S

- Find out where the nearest national or military cemetery is located close to your house and make plans to visit there on the next Memorial Day, Veterens Day, Flag Day, Fourth of July or other patriotic occasion.

- Look up addresses and phone numbers for your Congressmen and Senators. All of them have e-mails now. Write them a letter about an issue you feel strongly about. Thank them for the good they are doing.

- Research one of the service or humanitarian projects you have been thinking about donating to. Check out their web site and find out how you can get involved.

- Take treats to your local firemen. Thank them for the service they provide to your community.

- Find out what you need to do to start a Neighborhood Watch in your area. Call the local police department and talk to your neighbors.

"On the Sabbath days, as far as I am concerned, between the hours of service, I would love to have the privilege of sitting down in my home with my family and conversing with them, and visiting with them, and becoming better acquainted with them. I would like to have the privilege of occupying as much time as I could conveniently on the Sabbath day for this purpose; to get acquainted with my children, keep in touch with them, and to keep them in touch with the scriptures, and to think of something besides fun and jokes and laughter and merriment, and such things as these."

—President Joseph F. Smith

Messages of the First Presidency of the Church of Jesus Christ of Latter-day Saints, 6 vols, 1967-75, 5:17-18

IDEAS

- Go to the nearest animal shelter and volunteer to help play with the animals.

- Clean up garbage around a local park or playground.

- Take a bag of safe toys to a homeless shelter.

- Make an accounting of your tithing. Find out if you're caught up. Check your fast offering donations also.

- Learn about the Church's Perpetual Education fund. Fill out a donation slip and give it to the Bishopric.

- Find a service organization to support. Check out www.volunteermatch.org, www.networkforgood.org and www.pointsoflight.org, for ideas on potential projects and organizations.

Service

IDEAS

- Volunteer to use your house to host an evening where new members of the ward can meet the Bishopric and other auxiliary leaders.

- Offer to baby sit for free for a couple with children so they can afford to go out next weekend on a date.

- Invite a single mother and her children over to share Sunday dinner with you.

- If you have a cuddly or interesting pet that brings smiles to people's faces, call a local hospital or nursing home to see if you could bring your pet to share with patients.

- Tape record yourself reading the scriptures or the *Ensign* on cassette for someone who spends a lot of time in the car, for a person who can't see well, or for someone who is learning how to read.

- Do a secret service for someone.

"The manner in which we spend the Sabbath

is a sign of our inner attitude toward God."

—Elder Mark E. Peterson

Ensign, May 1975, p. 49

IDEAS

- Learn about the Presidential Service Award and earn it! It can be earned by individuals, by families, or even large groups working together.

- Write a note to someone you've noticed needs an encouraging word. Sign it "From someone who cares" and mail it.

- Visit someone who is sick or lonely.

- Invite a widow in your ward over for dinner. Find out if there are some "honey do" chores you could do to help her with her home during the next week.

- Think of a family service project. Find a nearby nursing home where you could volunteer to play board games or do crafts with the residents. You could also make an appointment to go one night for a fun Family Home Evening.

- Put together a care package for a missionary, someone in the military service, or someone who is away from home at school.

"The Sabbath is a holy day in which to do worthy and holy things. Abstinence from work and recreation is important but insufficient. The Sabbath calls for constructive thoughts and acts, and if one merely lounges about doing nothing on the Sabbath, he is breaking it. To observe it, one will be on his knees in prayer, preparing lessons, studying the gospel, meditating, visiting the ill and distressed, sleeping, reading wholesome material, and attending all the meetings of the day to which he is expected. To fail to do these proper things is a transgression on the omission side."

—Spencer W. Kimball
The Miracle of Forgiveness, 1969, p. 96-97

IDEAS

- Invite someone single to share dinner with your family.

- Ask your Bishop discreetly if there is someone in your ward who cannot afford a subscription to one of the Church magazines. You can write a check on Monday to pay for it anonymously and sign them up.

- Make Home Teaching and Visiting Teaching appointments.

- Make a week's worth of love notes you can slip into your family's lunchboxes, socks, shoes, drawers, briefcases, or other places during the week to surprise them.

- Plan a date when your family could clean the church building.

- Bring lunch or dinner to the Bishopric when they spend all day at church doing tithing settlements.

- Find the closest orphanage nearest you and make plans to visit it.

"Much of the sorrow and distress that is afflict-
ing and will continue to afflict mankind is trace-
able to the fact that they have ignored his (God's)
admonition to keep the Sabbath day holy."

—George Albert Smith

Conference Report, Oct. 1935, p. 120;
quoted by Ezra Taft Benson, *Ensign*, May 1971, p. 71

IDEAS

- Call the Relief Society Compassionate Service Leader in your Ward or Branch and ask how you could help.

- Visit someone in the hospital you know—or don't know.

- Make little food tray gifts for the hospital to put on the trays of patients who have been there a long time and need to feel loved and remembered.

- Take dinner to a shut-in or elderly person.

- Go with a priesthood holder to take the Sacrament to someone who is unable to attend Church.

- Think of someone who might need a ride to Church and offer to take them next Sunday.

- Volunteer to bring the snacks to the nursery next week whether you have young children or not.

- Volunteer to take home the nursery toys to clean or repair.

- Adopt a grandparent. Visit them on Sundays.

"The Lord has given the Sabbath day for your benefit and has commanded you to keep it holy. Many activities are appropriate for the Sabbath. Bear in mind, however, that Sunday is not a holiday. Sunday is a holy day."

—Thomas S. Monson
Ensign, Nov. 1990, p. 47

IDEAS

- Find out when the people you home teach or visit teach have birthdays and put those dates on your calendar. Plan to prepare something for them, whether it be a treat or card.

- Ask your Bishop or Relief Society President for the name of someone you could do anonymous service for. Then every Sunday spend time writing her letters, creating small gifts, or baking goodies.

- Drive a Deacon around to collect fast offerings for your ward or branch.

- Call your Visiting Teaching or Home Teaching Supervisor to give him or her your monthly report.

- Call or visit the people on your Visiting Teaching or Home teaching route again.

- Practice "pure religion" by visiting the "fatherless and widows in their affliction."

Church Preparation

IDEAS

- Read next week's Sunday School lesson! Find out what the assignment is and then go to church next week prepared to participate in the lesson.

- Read next Sunday's Relief Society's lesson or review the lesson you just heard today. You've probably heard the teacher say, "I don't have time to read this part, but go home and read it yourself because it's really good!"

- Read next Sunday's Priesthood lesson. The quorums are supposed to coordinate their material with the Relief Society's lesson so you can actually discuss it with your spouse. How can you apply today's lesson to improving your marriage and family life?

- Talk with your family about the lessons you had in Church today and what you learned.

"A world without a Sabbath would be like a man without a smile, like a summer without flowers, and like a homestead without a garden. It is the joyous day of the whole week."

—Henry Ward Beecher

Ensign, May 1971, p. 4

IDEAS

- Designate a box or begin a file where you can collect all of the handouts you get from Church to use in future talks and lessons.

- If your calling involves teaching, make nice handouts for your next lesson.

- Do an activity based on your child's Primary lesson of the day. Talk to his Primary teacher to find out what the lesson schedule is. Lessons can also be found at www.lds.org

- Offer to teach a lesson for a teacher who is planning to go on vacation.

- Prepare a Primary lesson you could give if a class is unexpectantly left without a teacher. Keep your lesson material in your Sunday bag or car so you can help out on a moment's notice.

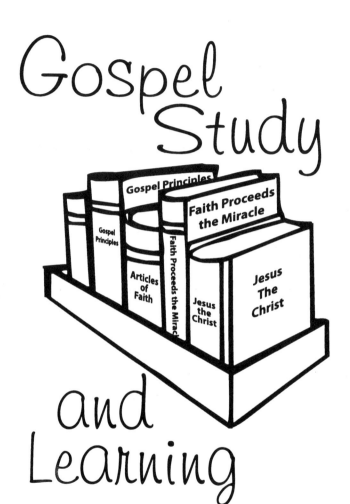

Gospel Study
and Learning

Gospel Principles
Faith Proceeds the Miracle
Gospel Principles
Articles of Faith
Faith Proceeds the Miracle
Jesus the Christ
Jesus The Christ

IDEAS

- Read and study your patriarchal blessing. If you don't have one yet, begin preparing yourself spiritually to receive one.

- Read a book about Christ's second coming. Outline the book of Revelation. Do you understand the timeline of the last days? Think about what you need to do to be better prepared for the Savior's return.

- Make a list of all the qualities of Jesus. Evaluate how you are doing. Write down what you can do to become more like him.

- Learn about a General Authority or Apostle of the Church. Learn about his life and read articles or talks he has written.

- Memorize all of the Articles of Faith.

- Memorize the Relief Society mission statement.

- Memorize the Oath and Covenant of the Priesthood found in D&C 84.

"Sunday is the golden clasp that binds together the volume of the week."

—Henry W. Longfellow

Ensign, May 1971, p. 4

IDEAS

- Memorize the Young Women's Statement.

- Memorize the Primary's "My Gospel Standards."

- Get large butcher paper to draw a time line of the scriptures, Church history, or a Prophet's life.

- Prepare a "Devotional" book that teenagers can use for Seminary when it's their turn to share a faith-promoting story, quote or poem.

- Study the Sacrament prayers for greater meaning and understanding. Memorize them.

- Get copies of the Seminary or Institute manual study guides to direct your own studies better. Find out if you could attend a class.

- Study the promises of Abraham and how his blessings relate to your patriarchal blessing.

- Write a modern day parable.

"I often wonder what happened to the good old saying 'Sunday best.' If our dress deteriorates to everyday attire, our actions seem to follow the type of the clothing we wear Of course, we would not expect our children to remain dressed in their church clothes all day, but neither would we expect them to dress in clothes that would not be appropriate for the Sabbath."

—Elder L. Tom Perry
Ensign, November 1984, p. 19

IDEAS

- Learn about the Dead Sea Scrolls. Find out if some of the replicas are being displayed nearby and make plans to see them.

- Write an article about some aspect of the gospel that you feel passionate about and submit it to one of the Church magazines for publication.

- Choose a gospel topic to become an expert in. Research everything you can about it.

- Reflect on the Word of Wisdom and how you could live the spirit of that law better. Learn about how to keep your body more healthy and strong.

- Study the Church's "The Living Christ" document.

- Study the Church's "Proclamation on the Family."

- Have children prepare short talks and practice giving them to the family for a Sunday evening family fireside.

"Because we live in a Sabbath-breaking society, we must—if we would magnify our callings in the priesthood—live in the world but not be of the world, for the Lord has said,'...the inhabitants of Zion shall...observe the Sabbath day to keep it holy.' (D&C 68:29.) If we are really intent on magnifying our callings in the priesthood, we will on the Sabbath day live within the framework of the instructions given by the Lord in that section of the Doctrine and Covenants."

—Marion G. Romney
Conference Report, April 1974, pp 116-117

IDEAS

- Read biographies of Church leaders and other inspirational people.

- Read a book about child development. Evaluate how you can help your child progress.

- Read the reports and talks given during the most recent General Conference. Have you applied their counsel to your life during the last six months?

- Choose a picture from the Church's Gospel Art Picture Kit to display in your home during the week. Read the accompanying scripture and learn about the context of the verse.

- Receive a father's blessing. Study the scriptures where other father's blessings are recorded.

- Learn more about Church history.

- Find out when the next BYU Education Week is and try to make plans to attend next year!

"Can we possibly imagine how tempting it must have been for our pioneer forefathers to break the Sabbath day? Their survival depended upon the food they could grow and harvest. Yet their leaders counseled them to exercise faith in the promises of the Lord and to respect the Sabbath day. Church members are the beneficiaries of that heritage and of the promises of the Lord to those who are faithful. We must always remember who we are and that we are different from the world."

—Elder Earl C. Tingey
Ensign, May 1966, p. 10

IDEAS

- Find out where the nearest Church's Visitors Centers or monuments are to your house. Plan a trip to go see them.

- Talk about how we share our testimonies at Church, work, or school. Practice sharing your testimony with others.

- Fast with purpose. Study scriptural accounts of people who fasted and why.

- Spend more time in prayer today. Really listen for answers.

- Keep a notebook of your prayers and how they were answered.

- Invite the Stake Patriarch and his wife over for dinner and have them share some of their uplifiting experiences with you.

Scripture Study

IDEAS

- Read the scriptures in another language. Whether you are already fluent in another tongue or just starting to learn, you'll find many new insights in the verses.

- Create a new code to mark your scriptures. You could put letters in the margins that represent certain themes. For example, put a "T" next to passages that provide insights into the temple or "M" next to missionary-related verses. Design your own symbols and you'll be amazed at how often your favorite subjects are taught.

- Mark a Book of Mormon to give to a friend. Highlight your favorite scriptures, Seminary Scripture Mastery verses, or scriptures used in the missionary discussions.

- Choose a scripture to memorize this week.

- Search the scriptures that relate specifically to your calling in the church. Decide what you need to do to "magnify your calling."

"True, Sunday is a day of rest, a change from the ordinary occupations of the week, but it is more than that. It is a day of worship, a day in which the spiritual life of man may be enriched. A day of indolence, a day of physical recuperation is too often a very different thing from the God-ordained day of rest. Physical exhaustion and indolence are incompatible with a spirit of worship. A proper observance of the duties and devotions of the Sabbath day will, by its change and its spiritual life, give the best rest that men can enjoy on the Sabbath day."

—President Joseph F. Smith
Teachings of Presidents of the Church:
Joseph F. Smith, p. 230

IDEAS

- Think about a specific problem you are having at work, school, or in your neighborhood. Study the scriptures to see how you should solve the problem.

- Make an accounting of your fast offerings. Study scriptures relating to offerings and reevaluate how much you give.

- Display your favorite scripture in your home by using your own artwork, calligraphy, cross stitch or some other creative way.

Developing and Sharing Talents

IDEAS

- Enter a local art or writing contest to share and improve your talents.

- Find out what contests will be held at your nearby county fair. See if you can share and improve your talents by entering a contest there.

- Develop and share some of your talents with your family.

- Enter one of the Church's literature or art contests. Begin working on your own masterpiece that will uplift and inspire other members.

- Write an uplifting story or personal experience that you could submit to the *Ensign* or one of the other Church magazines for publication.

- Write a skit that your family could perform at your next big family gathering or reunion.

"Since the Lord wants us to focus our Sabbath thoughts and actions on Him, it is only appropriate that we ask him to guide and bless these activities. In the words of Nephi, "Ye must not perform any thing unto the Lord save in the first place ye shall pray unto the Father in the name of Christ, that he will consecrate thy performance unto thee, that thy performance may be for the welfare of thy soul." (2 Nephi 32:9.) Prayer is an essential part of the refreshment and joy of the Sabbath."

—Karen Lynn
"Prayer: The Heart of the Sabbath,"
Ensign, Jan. 1978, p. 30

IDEAS

- Offer to be a guest speaker or teacher at a Cub Scout or Girl Scout meeting. Share one of your talents.

- Volunteer your talents and services to the Relief Society Enrichment leader. Offer to teach a class about something you know how to do well.

- Start writing that book you've always thought about writing.

- Check out community classes that are offered and develop a new talent!

Temple

IDEAS

- Review your temple worthiness and attendance.

- Invite someone to go with you to the temple next week or offer to baby-sit someone's children so they could go.

- Visit the nearest temple. Walk around the grounds. Take photos of your family in front of it.

- Make sure your temple recommend is updated. If not, make an appointment for an interview. Keep your recommend in your wallet as President Howard W. Hunter encouraged us to do.

- Start a sign up list to pass around in church for families that want to take turns babysitting each other's children so they can attend the temple.

- Learn about your favorite temple or the history of the temple closest to you. You can often find the dedicatory prayer on-line.

ABOUT THE AUTHOR

Trina Bates Boice grew up in sunny California and later braved the cold and snow at Brigham Young University, where she earned two bachelor's degrees. While at BYU she competed on the Speech and Debate team and the Ballroom Dance Team. She was president of the National Honor Society Phi Eta Sigma and served as ASBYU Secretary of Student Community Services.

Trina also studied at the University of Salamanca in Spain and later returned there to serve an LDS mission in Madrid. She also earned a master's degree from California College for Health Sciences. She worked as a legislative assistant for a congressman in Washington D.C. and wrote a column called "The Boice Box" for a newspaper in Georgia, where she lived for 15 years.

She has a real estate license, travel agent license, a Black Belt in Tae Kwon Do, and helps her husband, Tom, with their real estate appraisal and investment companies.

Trina is the "2004 Young Mother of the Year" for the state of California and lives in beautiful Carlsbad with Tom and their four sons, Cooper, Calvin, Bradley, and Bowen.